20TH CENTURY DESIGN
1900-20
THE BIRTH OF MODERNISM

For a free color catalog describing Gareth Stevens Publishing's list of high-quality books and multimedia programs, call 1-800-542-2595 (USA) or 1-800-461-9120 (Canada). Gareth Stevens Publishing's Fax: (414) 332-3567.

Library of Congress Cataloging-in-Publication Data available upon request from publisher. Fax: (414) 332-3567 for the attention of the Publishing Records Department.

ISBN 0-8368-2705-8

This North American edition first published in 2000 by
Gareth Stevens Publishing
A World Almanac Education Group Company
330 West Olive Street, Suite 100
Milwaukee, Wisconsin 53212 USA

Original edition © 1999 by David West Children's Books. First published in Great Britain in 1999 by Heinemann Library, Halley Court, Jordan Hill, Oxford OX2 8EJ, a division of Reed Educational and Professional Publishing Limited. This U.S. edition © 2000 by Gareth Stevens, Inc. Additional end matter © 2000 by Gareth Stevens, Inc.

Gareth Stevens Senior Editor: Dorothy L. Gibbs
Gareth Stevens Series Editor: Christy Steele

Picture Research: Brooks Krikler Research

Photo Credits:
Abbreviations: (t) top, (m) middle, (b) bottom, (l) left, (r) right

AKG London: Cover (bl, lm, mr), pages 3(l), 7(b), 8-9, 10(t), 11(br), 12(b), 15(b), 16(t), 16-17, 19(tr, br), 20-21, 21(tl), 24(bl), 29(b) / Peter Behrens © DACS 1999: page 28(l).
Corbis: Cover (rm, tr), pages 3(m, r), 4-5(b), 5(l), 8(both), 9(both), 10(b), 11(t), 12(l), 12-13, 13, 14(t, m), 15(tl, tr), 16(bl), 18(all), 19(tl, bl), 20(bl), 24-25(b), 25(t) / Bettmann: page 23(t) / UPI: pages 5(tr), 22(l).
Tom Donovan Military Pictures: page 4(m).
Mary Evans Picture Library: pages 6(tr), 6-7, 21(tr), 22(tr, br), 24-25(t), 25(b), 29(t).
Hulton Getty Collection: page 23(b).
© Hunterian Art Gallery, University of Glasgow, Mackintosh Collection: pages 14(b), 17(t).
Philip Jarrett: pages 26-27, 27(both).
Solution Pictures: Cover (br), pages 4-5(t), 26(m, bl, br).
Frank Spooner Pictures: Cover (tl), page 7(t) / Roger Viollet Collection: pages 6(tl), 11(bl).
Vitra Design Museum: pages 5(br), 17(b).
Reproduced by the kind permission of the London Transport Museum: page 28(r).

Printed in Mexico

1 2 3 4 5 6 7 8 9 04 03 02 01 00

20TH CENTURY DESIGN

1900-20

THE BIRTH OF MODERNISM

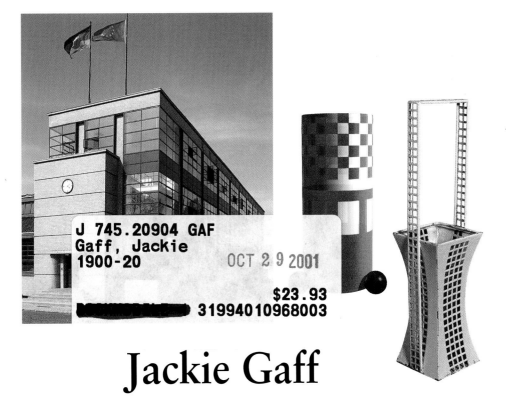

Jackie Gaff

Gareth Stevens Publishing
A WORLD ALMANAC EDUCATION GROUP COMPANY

CONTENTS

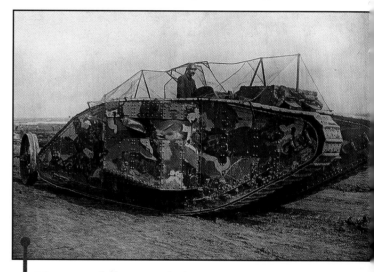

The invention of the gasoline engine in the 19th century made powered flight possible in the 20th century. The first powered plane, the Wright brothers' Flyer, took off in 1903.

Territorial disputes led to the outbreak of World War I in 1914. The first armored tanks went into battle in 1916. By the end of the war in 1918, about eight million troops had been killed.

Often, many years pass before new inventions replace outdated technology. In 1915, horse-drawn carriages still shared the streets of New York City with the new automobiles.

THE NEW CENTURY

Change rarely happens overnight. Despite the many remarkable inventions of the 19th century, including the electric motor and the gasoline engine, it was not until the first two decades of the 20th century that new technology began to replace the old. When better ways of making the new products lowered prices, new technology started to change people's lives.

Along with the devastation of World War I (1914–1918) came a new equality. While men from all walks of life were fighting side by side, women took over the men's jobs at home, earning new social and financial freedoms.

Although art and architecture in 1900 celebrated the ornate curves and stylized natural imagery of art nouveau, by 1920, radical artists, designers, and architects had started an artistic revolution. They turned away from the world of nature reflected in art nouveau and found new inspiration exploring abstract, geometric forms.

This electric lamp by Louis Comfort Tiffany has graceful art nouveau curves, a style that was popular in 1900.

The new century brought an explosion of new electrical devices that would transform life at home and at work.

By 1920, a less decorative, abstract style had emerged. (Red and Blue armchair by Gerrit Rietveld, 1918)

FASHIONABLE FINERY

The first few years of the new century saw little change in the formal rules of proper middle-class fashion. Men and women had to wear the correct outfits for morning, afternoon, and evening. They also had a variety of costumes, each one specifically designed for an activity, such as walking or riding in an automobile.

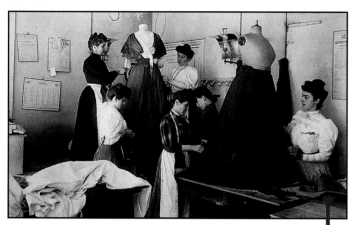

Although sewing machines were invented in the 19th century, most clothes in the early 20th century were still sewn by hand.

This woman's curvy, "S-bend" figure and elegant walking costume were the height of fashion in the early 1900s.

CHIFFON AND LACE

Clothing made of rustling chiffon and lace gave fashionable women a soft, feminine image. Necklines for evening wear were low, but skirts were long and full to prevent an unfashionable glimpse of ankle or calf.

UNDERCOVER STORY

Underneath their soft chiffons, women wore layers of elaborate undergarments and heavily boned corsets to shape their bodies. A tightly laced corset thrust out the bottom, pulled in the waist, and pushed out the bust to mold a woman's body into the fashionable female silhouette known as the "S-bend."

Women's fashions began to loosen up a little around 1910, as shown by the gowns in this painting of a ball held at London's Savoy Hotel in 1912.

NEWFOUND FREEDOMS

In the 1890s, women in New Zealand and in three American states won the right to vote. Through the early 1900s, suffragettes campaigned to extend this right to all women. Along with newfound political freedom came new freedom in fashion. Women gradually abandoned corsets for unboned stays and, by 1910, a straighter, less curvy silhouette was coming into vogue. The exotic oriental-style costumes designed by Léon Bakst (1866–1924) for the Russian Ballet greatly influenced these more relaxed fashions. The Ballet caused a sensation when it first performed in Paris in 1909.

Poiret's collections from 1911–1913 featured pantaloon dresses. The one in the center has a "lampshade" tunic.

POIRET ON THE LOOSE

If any one person was responsible for loosening up women's fashions, it was French couturier Paul Poiret (1879–1944). In 1906, he designed a simple, loose, high-waisted dress, and his 1909 collection featured harem pants inspired by the Russian Ballet. Poiret introduced his "lampshade" tunic in 1911.

WEARING THE PANTS

War work required functional clothing, so, for the first time, wearing pants was considered acceptable for Western women. Jodhpurs were practical for farmwork, and women wore boiler suits for some factory jobs. The new experience of working women changed attitudes toward women's clothing forever.

Not all of Poiret's designs were loose-fitting. His "hobble skirt" of 1911 was so narrow at the ankle that a woman could take only tiny steps in it.

ART NOUVEAU

French for "new art," *art nouveau* was a new style developed in the 1880s to replace the prevailing "old style," which was inspired by the art and designs of the past. With the approach of the new century, some artists and architects began to look forward for inspiration and developed modern styles for the modern age.

LEARNING THE LINES

At the heart of art nouveau style were its long, winding, flowing lines and a sense of lightness and grace. Artists drew images inspired mainly by the natural world. These images ranged from curling tendrils of vines and twisting locks of hair to peacocks, dragonflies, snakes, greyhounds, bats, irises, orchids, and lilies.

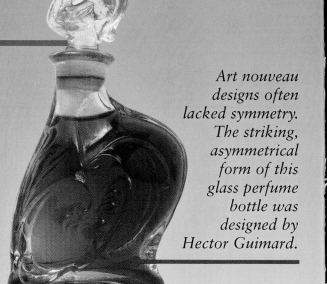

Art nouveau designs often lacked symmetry. The striking, asymmetrical form of this glass perfume bottle was designed by Hector Guimard.

The swirling lines of Czech painter Alphonse Mucha's (1860–1939) artwork are an excellent example of art nouveau style. This poster was designed in 1898.

8

FANNING THE FLAMES

Art nouveau spread like wildfire, promoted by international exhibitions and art journals, such as *The Studio*. In Germany, the new style was called *Jugendstil*, or "young style," after *Jugend* magazine. Unique interpretations of art nouveau developed in various cities — Paris and Nancy in France; Munich, Berlin, and Darmstadt in Germany; Brussels in Belgium; Barcelona in Spain; Glasgow in Scotland; Vienna in Austria; and New York City and Chicago in the United States.

French architect and designer Hector Guimard is best known for the fantastical plantlike forms he created for the Paris Métro system in 1903.

SIMPLIFYING THE LOOK

The swirling, curving lines of art nouveau, featured in works by Hector Guimard (1867–1942) of Paris and Antonio Gaudí (1852–1926) of Barcelona, remained popular well into the early 1900s. As art nouveau matured, however, a new style evolved. Inspired by Charles Rennie Mackintosh (1868–1928) of Glasgow, other designers began to explore straight lines and geometric forms.

Belgian architect and designer Henry van de Velde (1863–1957) rejected plant and animal motifs in favor of curving, abstract patterns like those on these stained-glass windows from the late 1890s.

GLASS MASTERS

Light, airy, delicate glass was an ideal material for art nouveau designs. Master craftsmen, such as Frenchman Emile Gallé (1846–1904) and American Louis Comfort Tiffany (1848–1933), experimented with glass-making techniques. Gallé opened his glassworks in Nancy, France, in 1874, while Tiffany opened his workshops on Long Island, New York, in 1893. Many of Tiffany's pieces glow with an iridescent metallic finish, created by spraying metallic chlorides on the glass.

Tiffany created magical stained-glass lamp shades like the one on this poppy table lamp with a bronze base.

9

NEW ARCHITECTURE

Architects were some of the first artists to create new styles for the modern age. In the 1890s and early 1900s, in cities throughout Europe, they designed some astonishing art nouveau buildings that were original not only in style, but also in the way they were constructed.

Like Charles Rennie Mackintosh, designer Josef Hoffmann used abstract, geometric forms. (The Palais Stoclet in Brussels, 1905–1911)

INDUSTRIAL MATERIALS

After development, in the 19th century, of techniques for mass-producing cast and wrought iron, engineers who constructed public buildings, such as train stations, used iron to create magnificent effects. Iron provided a strong and comparatively light framework, yet architects rarely used it. Even when they did, they hid the iron behind the brick and stonework of their designs. Art nouveau architects, however, excited by the decorative potential of iron, not only used it in the construction of their buildings, but also left it exposed to view.

With its clean lines and stark pebbledash exterior, designed by Charles Rennie Mackintosh, Hill House, at Helensburgh, near Glasglow, looked ultramodern in the early 1900s. (1902–1903)

10

LONE GENIUS

American Frank Lloyd Wright (1857–1959) was one of the new century's most innovative architects. His work had an enormous impact on architecture around the world. Throughout his long career, Wright avoided current styles and pursued his own personal vision. He loved using natural materials, such as wood, saying that he aimed to build "organic architecture" — buildings that seemed to grow naturally out of the landscape.

Frank Lloyd Wright was well known in the early 1900s for his Prairie Houses, which he designed to have low, horizontal exteriors, projecting roofs, and open-plan interiors. (Robie House in Chicago, 1909)

DECORATIVE IRONWORK

One of the first art nouveau architects to decorate with iron was Victor Horta (1861–1947) of Belgium. In his design for the Hôtel Tassel, the internal iron columns that carried much of the building's weight were exposed. Horta also had the iron molded into fantastical plant-stem shapes, complete with twining fronds.

Antonio Gaudí once said that there are no straight lines in nature, and his undulating Casa Batlló looks more like a lizard than an apartment building. (Barcelona, 1904–1906)

Decorative ironwork was used on the windows of Victor Horta's Hôtel Tassel. (Brussels, 1892)

TWISTING TRENDS

Horta and the extraordinary Spanish architect Antonio Gaudí developed the more curving, twisting art nouveau style. Other designers, such as Scotland's Charles Rennie Mackintosh and Austria's Josef Hoffmann (1870–1956), created a less ornate style, using straight, horizontal and vertical lines. The great American architect Frank Lloyd Wright was also passionate about straight lines, but Wright's work was so individual that it usually is not considered part of the art nouveau movement.

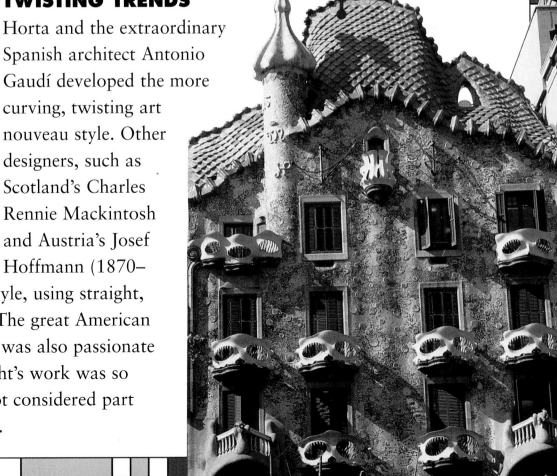

INDUSTRIAL ART

The development of industrial manufacturing during the 1800s brought on a flood of poorly designed products that prompted a design revolt in the last decades of the 19th century.

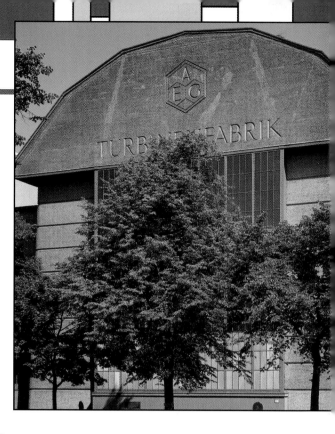

QUALITY CONTROL

For some architects and designers, this revolt meant a return to handcrafted goods made of natural materials, such as wood.

The Lingotto car factory, designed for Fiat by Italian engineer Matté Truco, was a reinforced-concrete masterpiece. (Turin, 1915)

For others, it meant forging closer links between art and industry, using modern technology and modern materials, such as reinforced concrete and steel, to create well-designed products. Of course, some designers wanted to do both!

GROUP WORK

Organizations, such as the Vienna Workshops and the Deutsche Werkbund (a German work association founded in 1907), formed to unite business and industry with arts and crafts. One of the cofounders of the Deutsche Werkbund was German architect and designer Peter Behrens (1868–1940). Behrens was among the first to design specifically for industry.

The boxlike Fagus shoe factory is one of the earliest examples of the modernist style that flourished after World War I. German-born architects Walter Gropius (1883–1969) and Adolf Meyer (1881–1929) designed it in 1910.

12

DESIGNING FOR INDUSTRY

Behrens worked mainly with handcrafted goods until 1907, when he was appointed design consultant to AEG, a German electrical company, styling the company's publications, products, and factories. Behrens's work, and the work of other designers, began to gradually shift away from the nature-inspired imagery of art nouveau toward simple, undecorated, geometrical buildings and objects that seemed to symbolize the modern age. By the 1930s, this new style was known as modernism.

Peter Behrens created this starkly simple design for AEG's turbine factory in 1908–1909.

THE AMERICAN REVOLUTION

Mass production of steel in Britain, Germany, and the United States in the 1850s to 1870s led to changes in construction methods that made buildings more than 1,300 feet (400 meters) high possible. In 1883, architect William Jenney (1832–1907) designed Chicago's Home Insurance Building using a metal framework instead of load-bearing walls to hold the weight. The Tacoma Building in Chicago, designed in 1887, was the first building with an all-steel skeleton.

Steel-girder skeleton

Non-load-bearing walls

In Chicago, architects explored design possibilities for skyscrapers, using strong, vertical lines and large windows. (Reliance Building, (1890–1894)

NDOOR STYLE

Victorian rooms were cluttered and gloomy. Furniture and windows were swathed in heavy, elaborate fabrics, and color schemes were bold and dark. Art nouveau interiors were just the opposite — simple, spacious, and filled with light. The difference was due largely to the new approach taken by architects and designers in the late 19th century.

14

A TOTAL LOOK

No longer content with designing only the structure and exterior of a building,

Frank Lloyd Wright pioneered the removal of internal walls to create open-plan interiors. He designed rooms that flowed out into the natural landscape. (Hollyhock House in Los Angeles, 1918)

architects began to style every aspect of the interior, from the colors of the walls to the shapes of chairs and door handles. A building and its contents became a single, harmonized work of art. As Frank Lloyd Wright explained, "It is quite impossible to consider the building as one thing, its furnishings another, and its setting and environment still another."

Charles Rennie Mackintosh and designer Margaret Macdonald, his wife, often worked together on design components, such as these doors in Glasgow's Willow Tea Rooms (1903–1905).

In 1906, Mackintosh and his wife designed simple, light-filled, white interiors for their own home.

In 1905–1906, Frank Lloyd Wright designed Unity Temple in Oak Park, Illinois. He styled every facet of the church's interior, including its sculptured electric lights.

Like Frank Lloyd Wright, American brothers Charles (1868–1957) and Henry (1870–1954) Greene created open-plan interiors and liked to work with natural materials, especially wood. (Gamble House in California, 1907–1908)

15

LETTING IN THE LIGHT

Art nouveau architects flooded rooms with light by increasing the size of windows and using skylights and the new electric lights invented in the 1870s. Stained-glass panels filtered daylight in softly glowing colors onto walls painted white or light shades of gray, olive, or mauve. Mauve was a color only recently made available through technology. For thousands of years, dyes were made from natural materials. Purple dye had been extracted from shellfish, but the process was difficult, making the color so rare it was reserved for royalty. British chemist Sir William Perkin (1838–1907) made the first synthetic dye, mauveine, in 1856, but it was not fashionable until the 1890s.

The extraordinary Antonio Gaudí turned the inside of his Casa Milá into an underwater grotto. (Barcelona, 1905–1910)

FURNITURE

Art nouveau architects designed interiors to match the sinuous curves on the exteriors of their buildings. The most excessive pieces of art nouveau furniture resembled flowering bushes, with feet that looked like roots and frameworks carved into the shapes of trunks and branches crowned with blossoming flowers.

In designing his own Brussels home in 1898–1901, Belgian architect Victor Horta made every last object swirl with elegant art nouveau style.

16

CREATING A TOTAL LOOK

Beetles, dragonflies, and other insects were favorite art nouveau motifs. The wildly inventive Italian designer and furniture maker Carlo Bugatti (1856–1940) created an entire Snail Room! The idea of designing a room to achieve a total look was an early 20th-century innovation. In the past, a variety of styles was jumbled together without a common theme.

The designs of Italy's Carlo Bugatti equaled those of Spain's Antonio Gaudí in eccentricity. This bizarre creation is a wooden cabinet!

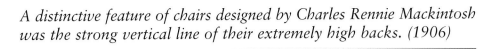

LEADING LIGHTS

Famous furniture designers of the period included Emile Gallé and Louis Majorelle (1859–1926) in France and Victor Horta and Henry van de Velde in Belgium. By the early 1900s, van de Velde had moved to a less decorative art nouveau style. He began to use simpler lines and forms, no longer believing that an object should reflect the world of nature. Instead, he believed that true beauty lay in usefulness rather than in decoration.

CLEANING UP THE ACT

Charles Rennie Mackintosh was one of the most influential designers in the trend toward simplification. His furniture was not just plain, it was severe — and, quite often, very uncomfortable. Unlike Henry van de Velde, Mackintosh was more concerned with shape than with usefulness or comfort.

By the early 1900s, Henry van de Velde, one of the founders of the Deutsche Werkbund, was designing simple, functional furniture.

Gerrit Rietveld's Red and Blue armchair (1918)

CUBIST CHAIR

Perhaps the most extreme example of shape before comfort was this chair created by Dutchman Gerrit Rietveld (1888–1964). Architects and designers were part of a wide-ranging art movement, and Rietveld's chair reflects the interest in primary colors and geometric shapes being explored by cubist painters such as Piet Mondrian (1872–1944).

17

THE VIENNA WORKSHOPS

The Vienna Workshops, or Wiener Werkstätte, was a group of more than ninety artists and craftsworkers, organized in 1903 by architect and designer Josef Hoffmann and painter Koloman Moser (1868–1918). According to Hoffmann, the Workshops' aim was to develop "an intimate relationship between the public, the designer, and the craftsman and to create good, simple things for the home."

The fashion studios made accessories, too, such as this handbag (c. 1910).

This 1917 poster for Vienna Workshops' fashions was designed by a leading member of the group, Dagobert Peche (1887–1923).

DESIGN STUDIOS

18

The Vienna Workshops consisted of a number of small studios that produced expensive, high-quality, handcrafted goods made from luxury materials. Different studios specialized in different arts, including furniture, metalwork, glassware, ceramics and pottery, bookbinding, jewelry, and, after 1910, clothing and fashion accessories. Like many artists and designers of the time, the Workshops' members rejected historical styles and created new ones. The group's early designs were greatly influenced by the simple, geometric style of Charles Rennie Mackintosh, who had visited Vienna in 1900.

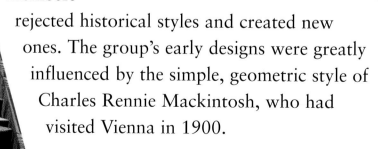

The Workshops left no corner of the home unstyled! This wooden toy town dates back to about 1918.

Austrian painter Gustav Klimt (1862–1918) was closely connected to the Vienna Workshops. He helped with fashion designs and created mosaic wall murals. Klimt also painted portraits of some of the Workshops' members, such as Emilie Flöge (1902).

ARTS AND CRAFTS MOVEMENT

The Vienna Workshops was just one of many associations inspired by the English arts and crafts movement of the mid-1850s. Led by idealists, such as poet William Morris (1834–1896), this movement opposed mass production, seeking to revive the importance of craftsmanship.

Geometric checks were a favorite motif in the Workshops' early years. (vase by Jutta Sika, c. 1905)

MASS-MARKET DESIGN

Although the arts and crafts movement believed that well-designed, quality goods should be available to all, only the wealthy could afford the Workshops' handmade products. Widespread availability was not achieved until people like Peter Behrens, who had belonged to an arts and crafts group in the early 1900s, began designing for mass production.

The severity of this metal basket by Josef Hoffmann (c. 1905) was meant to be softened with a potted plant.

19

STYLE SETTER
Like many architects of the time, Josef Hoffmann was interested in all aspects of design, styling everything from furniture and glassware to carpets and cutlery. Instead of drawing upon the natural world for imagery, Hoffmann focused on geometric shapes, earning the nickname *Quadratl,* or "Little Square." Hoffmann's work influenced the purely geometric styles of the 1920s and 1930s.

Hoffmann liked to contrast his use of line with circular motifs and real plants. (sketch of an interior, 1899)

TURNING THE TABLES

Like furniture designs of the early 20th century, styles of glassware and other tableware ranged from the ornate art nouveau of Louis Comfort Tiffany to the more restrained, geometric patterns of Josef Hoffmann and the Vienna Workshops. Some artists continued to focus on handcrafted objects, but others deliberately began to design for mass production.

THE STORY OF GLASS

Technological developments helped revolutionize the production of glassware. The art of glassblowing started in the Middle East in about 100 B.C. The process involved a glassmaker blowing air down a narrow metal tube into a lump of molten glass. This technique remained unchanged until the late 19th century, when people began to experiment with using machine-compressed air instead of blowing air by mouth.

Frank Lloyd Wright explored the use of abstract forms. In 1915–1922, he designed this porcelain place setting for the Imperial Hotel in Tokyo.

Josef Hoffmann was one of the designers who continued to create objects to be handcrafted. The delicate designs on this decorative glassware (c. 1912) were hand-painted.

A machine could never create the swirling colors and shapes seen in this Jack-in-the-Pulpit vase by Louis Comfort Tiffany (c. 1912).

MACHINES TAKE OVER

By 1907, machines were making bottles and other glassware automatically. Machines did everything from mixing and firing raw materials to molding and shaping bottles to annealing, or heat treating. Production rates rose from 200 bottles an hour in the 1880s to 2,500 bottles an hour — and prices dropped! With similar developments occurring in other industries, affordable, functional tableware became more widely available.

The Coca-Cola bottle is probably the world's most famous piece of packaging. The drink was invented in 1886, and the bottle was given its shape in 1915–1920.

New on the table in 1915, heat-resistant glassware was marketed by the American company Pyrex Corning.

NEW MATERIALS

More than just production methods were changing in the early 1900s; new materials were introduced, too. In 1914, the first stainless-steel knives were made in Sheffield for British scientist Harold Brearley (1871–1948). Brearley realized the commercial potential of this rust-resistant metal while investigating its use in making rifle barrels.

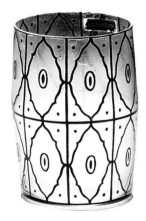

TURNING BOTTLE-MAKING UPSIDE DOWN

To make a bottle by machine, molten glass flows into a mold that has the bottle's neck and mouth at the bottom. Compressed air is blown in to push the molten glass up into the mold, forming a thick-walled bottle called a blank. The blank is turned right side up and put into a finishing mold. Compressed air is used again to blow the final shape.

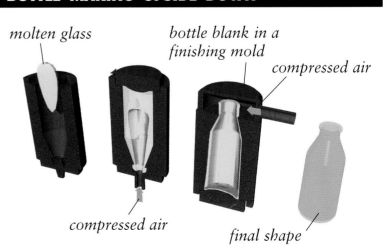

molten glass

bottle blank in a finishing mold

compressed air

compressed air

final shape

21

INNOVATIONS AT HOME

The technological development that had the greatest impact on home life in the early 20th century was electric power. The first power stations began operating in the 1880s, but, for the first few decades, only the wealthy could afford to have electricity in their homes. Affordability, however, did not hold back a flood of new electrical inventions.

THE FIRST DUST-BUSTERS

British engineer Hubert Booth (1871–1955) patented the first vacuum cleaner in 1901. A gasoline engine supplied the power for the machine to suck dust down long hoses into a horse-drawn cart parked outside the house. Portable electric vacuum cleaners were developed in the United States. William Hoover (1849–1932) was the first to market them in 1908.

Power connections in the early days of electricity could be unusual. This 1913 teamaker plugs into a light socket!

The servants of wealthy families were among the first to benefit from electrical innovations such as this floor polisher.

Early electrical devices were expensive, but mass production rapidly brought prices down. By the 1930s, Hoovers cost one-third less than in 1920.

The New **HOOVER**
It BEATS ... as it Sweeps   as it Cleans

By Appointment

The **HOOVER**

more d.p.m.
DIRT PER MINUTE
The accurate measure of electric cleaner efficiency

This electric kettle was designed by Peter Behrens for the German AEG company in 1909.

An easy way to shop for household goods was mail order. In the United States, Sears, Roebuck and Co. sent out its first mail-order catalog in 1896.

PRIVATE HOMES

Most middle- and upper-class 19th-century households relied on one or more live-in servants to do the cooking, cleaning, washing, and ironing by hand. By the 1910s, however, with more jobs to choose from, fewer people were choosing domestic service. As servants became less available, labor-saving electrical devices, such as the vacuum cleaner, filled the gap. Without live-in servants, the home evolved into a private space for the family.

Edison's phonograph could record and replay music. People could either buy cylinders or make their own.

MUSICAL MACHINES

By 1900, two kinds of record players were available: the phonograph invented by Thomas Edison (1847–1931) in 1877 and the gramophone trademarked by Emil Berliner (1851–1929) in 1894. The phonograph used cylinders coated with foil or wax. The gramophone used a flat disk, called a record, made from shellac, a natural plastic resin secreted by scale insects. By 1920, records had almost completely replaced cylinders.

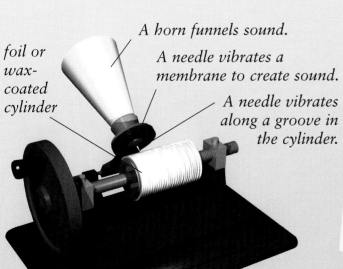

A horn funnels sound.

foil or wax-coated cylinder

A needle vibrates a membrane to create sound.

A needle vibrates along a groove in the cylinder.

23

TRANSPORTATION

Before 1900, people usually traveled by horse, bicycle, boat, train, and, most often, on foot. The new century brought new methods of transportation, with streetcars, buses, and underground train networks that branched out into the suburbs of every major city.

CHANGE OF POWER

In 1863, a steam locomotive pulled the first underground train, in London. Modern electric railway systems were not possible until 1879, when scientists demonstrated the first electric train, in Berlin. Implementing this new technology took even longer. Underground electric trains were not built in Europe or the United States until the late 1890s.

Another great 19th-century invention was the gasoline-fueled automobile, first made by German engineers Karl Benz (1844–1929), in 1885, and Gottlieb Daimler (1834–1900), in 1886.

"Griffon"

All early motorcycles were built by their inventors and were not sold to the public. The first motorcycle factory opened in Germany in 1894. The bike in this poster is from about 1905.

The first automobiles had no roofs, doors, or windshields. Passengers had to cover themselves from head to toe to keep off the dust and rain.

CUTTING COST

For many years, automobiles were so expensive to manufacture that only the wealthy could afford them. In 1901, however, the Oldsmobile Company started mass-producing them. In 1903, engineer Henry Ford (1863–1947) went a step further, founding his own automobile-manufacturing company in Detroit.

AUTOS FOR EVERYONE

Henry Ford wanted to build an automobile "so low in price that no man making a good salary will be unable to own one." In 1908, Ford launched his affordable Model T, but the major breakthrough in reducing cost came in 1913 when Ford put moving assembly lines into his factories. The time it took to make the chassis of a Model T Ford dropped from 728 minutes to 93 minutes!

Even in big cities like New York, it took a long time for automobiles to replace horse-drawn carriages. This street scene is from about 1915.

PUTTING THE PARTS TOGETHER

Henry Ford's assembly line made manufacturing faster and more efficient by breaking down the assembly process into a series of tasks. Each task was completed by a different person or machine as a traveling conveyor belt moved the car forward to each work station.

Ford's first automobiles rolled off his assembly line in 1913.

25

LOSS OF A TITAN
The *Titanic* was the largest, most luxurious ocean liner ever built and was believed to be the safest until it struck an iceberg on April 14, 1912 — and sank. More than 1,500 people died in the greatest transportation disaster the world had ever known.

The Titanic sank within three hours after hitting an iceberg.

FLYING MACHINES

The gasoline engine did more than transform land transportation — it opened the skies to powered flying machines. Although daring aviators had experimented with gliders and hang gliders during the 19th century, they had one big stumbling block to powered flight — the lack of a suitable engine.

THE WRIGHT *FLYER*

The first successful flight of a powered aircraft took place in the United States at Kitty Hawk, North Carolina. On a frosty morning in December 1903, a plane called *Flyer* made its first bumpy flight, which lasted for twelve seconds. This historic event was the work of the Wright brothers, Orville (1871–1948) and Wilbur (1867–1912). Their research tested full-size gliders in a home-built wind tunnel, and they made more than 1,000 glider flights. Finding an automobile engine too heavy for their aircraft, the brothers finally designed and built their own lightweight plane engine.

Flyer's *lightweight engine was mounted on the plane's lower wing.*

26

Flyer *carried only one pilot, who lay facedown beside the engine. Wilbur and Orville tossed a coin to decide who would fly first — Orville won.*

The Wright brothers designed and built bicycles before they became fascinated by flight in the 1890s.

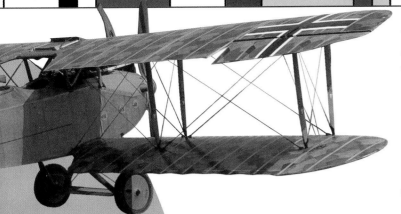

Alcock and Brown flew across the Atlantic Ocean in 16 hours and 12 minutes, winning fame and glory — and £10,000 from a newspaper.

RECORD-BREAKING DECADES

As engineers raced to build better and faster machines, aviators broke one flying record after another. In 1909, French pilot Louis Blériot was the first to fly across the English Channel. In June 1919, British pilots John Alcock and Arthur Brown made the first nonstop, transatlantic flight.

In 1919, converted wartime bombers began making commercial passenger flights.

MATERIAL GAINS

New flying records went hand in hand with technological advancements, and, around 1919, a big breakthrough came in the materials used for aircraft construction. A lightweight aluminum alloy, called duralumin, which was developed in 1908–1912, made practical, all-metal aircraft possible. Before 1919, most planes were made of wood and canvas.

THE POSITIVES OF PURE ALUMINUM

A new technique in the 1880s made the production of aluminum alloys in commercial quantities possible. This technique used electrolysis to obtain pure aluminum from alumina, or aluminum oxide. Molten alumina and an aluminum compound called cryolite are poured into a container. When an electric current is passed through the container, negatively-charged oxygen particles in the alumina move to the positive anodes, and positively-charged aluminum particles collect on the negative cathode floor beneath a layer of liquid cryolite. The pure aluminum can then be siphoned off.

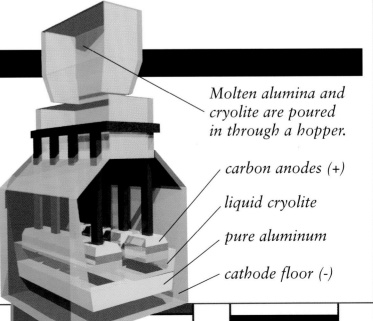

Molten alumina and cryolite are poured in through a hopper.

carbon anodes (+)

liquid cryolite

pure aluminum

cathode floor (-)

POSTERS & PRINTING

Technological advancements in printing revolutionized advertising around the turn of the century. Before the 1850s, most posters were type only, with an occasional woodcut picture. They were printed in a single color, usually black, and the design was very busy. By the 1900s, posters were pictorial and printed in a riot of colors.

® LRT

Peter Behrens designed this poster for a 1914 exhibition of Deutsche Werkbund products. The subtitle reads "Art in craft, industry and commerce • architecture."

Sans-serif typefaces have a simpler, cleaner look. A serif is a short stroke at the tip of a printed letter. Edward Johnston (1872–1944) designed this sans-serif typeface for the London Underground in 1916.

THE SCIENCE OF PRINTING

All this color resulted from the development of techniques, during the 19th century, for making multicolored prints — first by hand, then by machine. One of the most important technological advancements in machine printing was a process called offset lithography.

ROLLING THE PRESSES

Lithography is based on the chemical principle that oil and water do not mix. In offset lithography, a flexible, metal printing plate is wrapped around a printing cylinder. A grease-based ink is rolled onto the printing cylinder, which is dampened by water rollers. Images to be printed accept the greasy ink, while damp, non-image areas reject it. The inked images are then "offset" onto a rubber "blanket" roller and, from there, are transferred onto a sheet or roll of paper.

American Frederic Goudy (1865–1947) was a prolific type designer of the 20th century. One of his most successful typefaces was Goudy Old Style, designed in 1915.

1 2 3 4 5 6 7 8 9 0

A B C D E F G H I J K L M N O P Q R S T U V W X Y Z

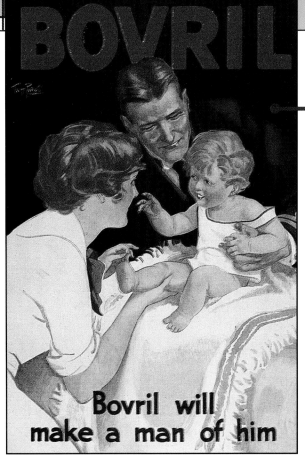

New marketing techniques accompanied developments in poster design. Advertising slogans, like the one on this poster from 1919, appeared during the late 1910s.

Another important advancement was mechanical typography. Before the invention of typesetting machines in the 1880s, typesetters placed each letter in every printed word by hand. Mechanical typesetting and color lithography meant that poster design could now be done by artists instead of by typesetters. Once again, new technology made new style possible.

THE ART OF POSTERS

French painter Henri de Toulouse-Lautrec (1864–1901), Czech Alphonse Mucha, and American Maxfield Parrish (1870–1966) were among the artists creating posters at the turn of the century. A single, striking image dominated the new look, with only a few words set in large, dramatic typefaces. Although people specially trained in drawing, printing, and lettering emerged early in the century, the term "graphic designer" was not used until the 1920s.

Poster designs of the period ranged from the cool formality of Peter Behrens's work to the bold emotionalism of this 1914 poster by Artur Berger.

29

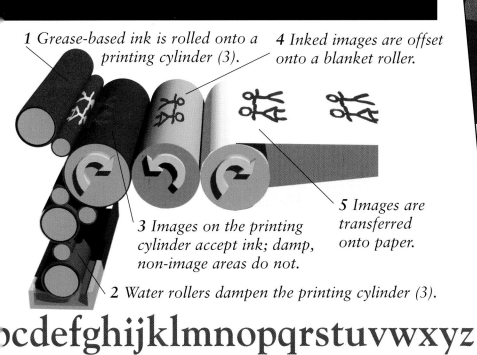

1 Grease-based ink is rolled onto a printing cylinder (3).

4 Inked images are offset onto a blanket roller.

3 Images on the printing cylinder accept ink; damp, non-image areas do not.

5 Images are transferred onto paper.

2 Water rollers dampen the printing cylinder (3).

bcdefghijklmnopqrstuvwxyz

· T I M E   L I N E ·

	DESIGN	WORLD EVENTS	TECHNOLOGY	FAMOUS PEOPLE	ART & MEDIA
1900	•Paris design exhibition celebrates art nouveau	•China: Boxer Rebellion •UK Labour Party formed	•First vacuum cleaner patented by Hubert Booth	•Freud: The Interpretation of Dreams	•Puccini: Tosca •Beatrix Potter: Peter Rabbit
1901		•Commonwealth of Australia proclaimed	•Marconi sends trans-atlantic morse code signal	•Death of Queen Victoria •President McKinley shot	•Chekhov: The Three Sisters •Rudyard Kipling: Kim
1902	•Carlo Bugatti: Snail Room	•South Africa: Second Boer War ends			•Georges Méliès's 14-minute film, A Trip to the Moon
1903	•Charles Rennie Mackintosh: Hill House	•UK: Women's Social and Political Union	•Wright brothers complete first powered flight	•Henry Ford founds Ford Motor Company in Detroit	•Jack London: Call of the Wild
1904		•Japan and Russia at war (to 1905)	•Autochrome color films patented by Lumière brothers		•Joseph Conrad: Nostromo •Synge: Riders to the Sea
1905	•Antonio Gaudí begins designing Casa Milá	•Norway gains independence from Sweden		•Albert Einstein: Special Theory of Relativity	
1906	•Paul Poiret loosens up fashions for women	•U.S.: San Francisco earthquake	•Enrico Forlanini tests first successful hydrofoil	•Theodore Roosevelt wins Nobel Peace Prize	
1907	•Behrens starts industrial design for AEG	•New Zealand acquires Dominion status	•First synthetic plastic, Bakelite, invented		•Picasso: first cubist art Les Demoiselles d'Avignon
1908		•Austria annexes Bosnia-Herzegovina	•Model T Ford launched •Hoover vacuum marketed	•Baden-Powell founds the Boy Scout Movement	•Matisse: The Dinner Table (Harmony in Red)
1909	•Frank Lloyd Wright: Robie House	•Young Turks overthrow Turkish Sultan		•Blériot flies across Channel •Russian Ballet visits Paris	•Strauss: Der Rosenkavalier
1910	•Gropius and Meyer: Fagus shoe factory	•Union of South Africa created	•Cellophane developed •First seaplane flight	•Death of Edward VII •Mother Teresa born	•Stravinsky: The Firebird •Kandinsky: Cossacks
1911	•Josef Hoffmann: Palais Stoclet	•Chinese revolution: emperor overthrown	•First motorized washing machine invented	•Roald Amundsen reaches the South Pole	
1912		•Balkan Wars (to 1913)	•Duralumin and stainless steel developed	•Robert Scott dies in Antarctica	•Ravel's Daphnis et Chloë first performed
1913			•Italy: First geothermal power station opens	•Suffragette Emily Davidson dies at the Derby	•Proust: Swann's Way
1914	•Deutsche Werkbund exhibition in Cologne	•Outbreak of World War I	•U.S.: First traffic lights	•Assassination of Archduke Franz Ferdinand in Sarajevo	•Charlie Chaplin's tramp appears in Kid Auto Races
1915	•Frederic Goudy designs Goudy Old Style type	•ANZAC troops slaughtered on Gallipoli	•Chemical weapons first used in warfare	•Death of Rupert Brooke	•Malevich: Eight Red Rectangles
1916	•Edward Johnston: Underground typeface	•Ireland: Easter Rising in Dublin	•Tanks first used in battle	•Margaret Sanger opens first birth-control clinic in U.S.	•D.W. Griffith: Intolerance •Kafka: Metamorphosis
1917		•Russian Revolution •USA enters World War I	•Clarence Birdseye starts deep-freezing foods	•Mata Hari executed as a spy	•Mary Pickford stars in Poor Little Rich Girl
1918	•Gerrit Rietveld: Red and Blue armchair	•World War I ends •UK: women get vote		•Russian tsar and his family are murdered	•Sassoon: Counterattack •Woolf: Night and Day
1919	•Bauhaus design school founded in Germany	•Treaty of Versailles •Nazi Party founded	•Ernest Rutherford splits the atom	•Alcock and Brown make first transatlantic flight	•Marcel Duchamp: Fountain

GLOSSARY

alloys: mixtures of two or more metals, or a metal and a nonmetal, made either by fusing them or melting them together.

cast iron: an alloy of iron, carbon, and silicon, particularly suitable for making molded objects because it solidifies to a hardness that cannot be bent even by a hammer, and it fuses more easily than steel.

cryolite: a white mineral containing sodium and aluminum, which is used as a source of aluminum.

cubist: related to a style of art that has an abstract, rather than pictorial, structure and often features fragmented forms of an object or several views of the same object.

duralumin: a strong, but lightweight, alloy made from about 94 percent aluminum mixed with small amounts of copper, manganese, and magnesium.

electrolysis: a process that produces chemical changes by passing an electric current through a dissolved substance, conveying ions to the positive (anode) and negative (cathode) terminals of an electrolytic cell.

mass production: the machine manufacturing of standardized products in large quantities.

reinforced concrete: concrete strengthened by having steel bars or wires embedded in it.

stainless steel: an alloy of about 74 percent steel mixed with chromium and nickel or molybdenum, which is extremely resistant to rust and corrosion.

symmetry: a proportional balance achieved when the opposite sides of an object reflect each other in size, shape, and position.

undulating: moving in a flowing, wavelike pattern or resembling waves.

MORE BOOKS TO READ

422 Art Nouveau Designs and Motifs in Full Color. Dover Pictorial Archive (series). Hans Anker and Julius Klinger (Dover Publications)

Art and Technology Through the Ages. Ideas That Changed the World (series). Jacqueline Dineen (Chelsea House)

Frank Lloyd Wright for Kids: His Life and Ideas. Kathleen Thorne-Thomsen (Chicago Review Press)

The Look of the Century: Design Icons of the 20th Century. Michael Tambini (Dorling Kindersley)

Skyscrapers. Andrew Dunn (Thomson Learning)

The Story of Flight. Voyages of Discovery (series). Dan Hagedorn and Sheila Keenan, editors (Scholastic)

Technology in Action. Designs in Science (series). Sally Morgan and Adrian Morgan (Facts on File)

Toilets, Toasters & Telephones: The How and Why of Everyday Objects. Susan Goldman (Browndeer Press)

Why Design? Activities and Projects from the National Building Museum. Anna Slafer and Kevin Cahill (Chicago Review Press)

WEB SITES

Art Nouveau Architecture. *www.greatbuildings.com/ types/styles/art_nouveau.html*

Fashion Trends and Cultural Influences 1900-1929. *udel.edu/~orzada/trends-29.htm*

The History of Invention. *www.cbc4kids.ca/general/ the-lab/history-of-invention/default.html*

The History of Printing. *www.usink.com/history_printing.html*

Due to the dynamic nature of the Internet, some web sites stay current longer than others. To find additional web sites, use a reliable search engine with one or more of the following keywords: *architecture, art nouveau, automobiles, cubism, Henry Ford, furniture, Gaudí, glassware, interior design, inventions, Frank Lloyd Wright,* and *Wright brothers.*

INDEX